DATE DUE			
FE 23 '88	OC 3 '92	JY 09 '04	
AP 21 '88	OC 10 '9	AG 30 '0	
AP 28 '88	DE 2 '9	OC 13 '10	
JE 23 '88	MR 31 '9		
JY 07 '88	NO 8 '9	MY 02 '1	
DE 13 '88	JAN 28 '94	AU 04 '22	
JA 5 '8	MAY 25 '94		
JE 23 '89	AUG 06 97		
FE 28 '90	EB 17 '8		
MY 17 '90	OC 27 '00		
JY 31 '91	JE 09 0		
NO 26 '91	JE 29 0		

MANUAL OF
THROWS
FOR SPORT JUDO AND
SELF-DEFENSE

MANUAL OF
THROWS
FOR SPORT JUDO AND
SELF-DEFENSE

Fred Neff

Photographs by James E. Reid

Lerner Publications Company
Minneapolis

The models photographed in this book are Mike Podolinsky, Rick Rowell, Bill Polta, and Laura Phillips.

LIBRARY OF CONGRESS CATALOGING IN PUBLICATION DATA

Neff, Fred.
Manual of throws for sport judo and self-defense.

(Fred Neff's Self-Defense Library)
Includes index.
SUMMARY: Describes with step-by-step instructions and photographs over 20 throws taken from sport judo and other Oriental fighting arts.

1. Judo. 2. Self-defense. [1. Judo. 2. Self-defense] I. Reid, James E. II. Title.

GV1114.N45   796.8'152   75-38476
ISBN 0-8225-1155-X

Manufactured in the United States of America

International Standard Book Number: 0-8225-1155-X
Library of Congress Catalog Card Number: 75-38476

3 4 5 6 7 8 9 10 92 91 90 89 88 87 86 85 84 83 82

CONTENTS

To Jason and Bradley Spellberg, in the hope that they grow up to be as good and kind as their grandfather, Elliott Neff

PREFACE

When I became a student of karate in the 1950's, few Americans had knowledge of the Oriental fighting arts or were interested in learning them. Since that time, however, public interest in the subject has grown considerably. Today, thousands of people all over the country are studying the various fighting arts and are learning that they offer many physical, psychological, and social benefits.

This new interest and involvement in the Oriental fighting arts has created a need for books that can be used as instructional guides for beginning students. FRED NEFF'S SELF-DEFENSE LIBRARY was written to help meet that need. My purpose in writing the series was to provide a basic comprehensive course on self-defense, based on the major Oriental disciplines of karate, judo, and jujitsu. In preparing each book, I was careful to include not only the physical techniques of Oriental fighting but also the underlying philosophical principles. This is important because an understanding of both elements is required of every martial arts student. Finally, in selecting the particular self-defense techniques for each book, I tried to include techniques that could be of practical use to the average person and that could be performed effectively and safely through practice. I genuinely hope that each and every reader of the SELF-DEFENSE LIBRARY benefits as much as I have from studying the martial arts.

I would like to express my thanks and appreciation to Mr. Harry Lerner, president of Lerner Publications Company, for his enthusiasm and support in the development of this series. I would also like to thank my students, who contributed their time and skill to demonstrating the various fighting techniques in the books. Finally, I would like to express special appreciation to the staff at Lerner Publications for its work in the production of the series.

Fred Neff

INTRODUCTION

If you mention the art of throwing to most people, they immediately think of movie or television heroes who flip huge attackers over their shoulders with a mere twist of the arm. Throwing techniques are staged to look so easy on the screen that most people don't realize how much ability it takes to perform them in a real situation. In reality, there are no "tricks" to throwing: the only thing that gives a person the ability to throw an opponent is genuine skill, acquired through years of instruction, practice, and experience. This book has been written to provide a proper groundwork for students who want to begin learning the exciting and challenging art of throwing.

The art of throwing was developed in the Orient over a period of many centuries. The ancient Chinese are generally credited with being the first people to develop formal throwing techniques for self-defense. The ancient Japanese people also developed a sophisticated self-defense system called *jujitsu*, which combined throwing techniques with punches, kicks, and holds. Jujitsu was used by Japanese samurai warriors for actual combat until the end of the 19th century, when the samurai way of fighting began to die out. At this point, a Japanese jujitsu expert named Dr. Jigoro Kano decided to adapt jujitsu techniques for use in sport competition rather than combat. In 1882, he introduced a new game called *judo*.

Judo was made up of holds, chokes, and throws taken from jujitsu. Dr. Kano chose only those techniques that would be both safe and effective for sport competition, and he refined these techniques to make them even safer. Dr. Kano's new game rapidly gained popularity, and today sport judo is practiced by enthusiastic students and professionals all over the world. Judo is so popular that it is now included in the international Olympic games.

In a sport judo contest, there are strict rules of conduct and etiquette. The contest takes place in a room in which the floors are covered with safety mats. A referee and judges preside over each match. At the beginning of the match, the two participants face each other and bow. Then, at a signal from the referee, they grasp each other's gis (GHEEZ), or jackets, and maneuver each other around on the mat until one sees an opportunity to off-balance and throw the other. In a judo match, points are awarded on the basis of correct form and power in executing throws. Contestants also gain points for successful holds or chokes. Only traditionally accepted judo throws, holds, and chokes are allowed; contestants may not kick or punch each other, or use throwing techniques that are not an accepted part of judo.

The throws presented in this book are taken largely from jujitsu and judo. Most of them are appropriate for both sport judo and self-defense. Others are not part of sport judo, but are an excellent means of practical self-defense. Whether you wish to train for sport judo or to learn throws for self-protection, the lessons in this book should provide a good basic introduction to the art of throwing.

COMMON QUESTIONS ABOUT THE ART OF THROWING

Because the art of throwing has received so much publicity in recent years, many people have become curious about how throwing is really done. The following section includes a brief overview of the principles of throwing, and attempts to answer some of the questions most commonly asked about this exciting art.

1. Is it actually possible for a small person to throw a larger, heavier opponent?

If a person uses proper throwing techniques, he or she can certainly throw a larger opponent. Success in throwing depends on skill and agility, not on physical size.

2. Does practicing the art of throwing help to make a person physically fit?

Practicing the art of throwing is an excellent way to condition the body and to improve overall coordination. Judo players are known not only for their throwing skill but also for their agility and excellent muscle condition.

3. How many throws must a person learn in order to win a judo match?

The winner of a judo match is not necessarily the person who knows the greatest number of throws; rather, it is the person who can use a few throws to the best advantage. It is better to know one throw perfectly than it is to be slightly familiar with many throws that you cannot do correctly in the appropriate situations.

4. Are throwing techniques more effective in a real self-defense situation than punching or kicking techniques?

No one fighting technique is superior to another in *all* self-defense situations: each technique has its own special advantages. Punches are fast techniques for close-in situations, and can be directed at any part of an aggressor's upper body. Kicks are very powerful and can be directed at an attacker from a safe distance. For close-in fighting against a strong attacker, one throw is often powerful enough to stop a fight. Because each technique has special advantages, it is best to use a combination of punches, kicks, and throws in a fight. In this way, the whole body can be used for self-defense.

5. When is the correct time to use fighting techniques in a real self-defense situation?

You should not use any fighting technique unless you are in immediate danger of being physically harmed. As a student of the art of throwing, your first responsibility is to avoid fights by exercising self-control, and by ignoring verbal threats and insults. A person skilled in the martial arts should never start a fight, and should always remember that along with strength and fighting skill comes a responsibility to show kindness and respect for other people.

6. What kinds of techniques help to make a throw successful?

Listed below are four elements that are essential parts of any successful throw. If you remember these concepts and use them at each practice session, you will greatly improve your throwing skill.

a. Make sure that your opponent is off balance before you attempt any throw.

b. Always get a firm grip on your opponent before throwing him or her.

c. Always begin a throw from the proper stance, or body position.

d. Execute each step of the throwing technique correctly, and try to perform the sequence of steps in one smooth, continuous motion. If your movements are smooth and flowing, you will gain the momentum you need to throw an opponent who is larger or stronger than you are.

7. How long does it take a student to learn how to throw any opponent successfully?

Throwing is a demanding art that requires many years of hard work, practice, and experience. Even with a lot of practice, there is no guarantee that you will be able to throw *every* opponent successfully. The skill of your opponent, as well as other factors, will always affect any throw that you attempt. The more you practice, however, the better will be your chances of performing throws successfully in any situation.

1.

WARM-UP EXERCISES FOR THROWING

This chapter describes a number of warm-up exercises that should be done at the beginning of every practice session. These exercises are essential to the art of throwing, because they strengthen and stretch the muscle groups that are used in doing the various throws. If you limber up before practice sessions, you will be able to perform strenuous throwing techniques more easily and with less risk of muscle injury. Constant exercise will also help you to achieve overall physical fitness. If you practice throwing several times a week and do warm-up exercises at each session, you will soon begin to look and feel healthy and physically fit.

Each of the exercises in this chapter should be repeated several times before every practice session. When first doing warm-up exercises, stretch your muscles only as far as they will go without strain. Too much stretching at the beginning may pull or tear the very muscles you are working so hard to condition. At first, you may not be able to copy exactly the positions shown in this chapter. But if you do a little stretching each day, you will soon be limber enough to do even the most difficult exercises correctly.

The Basic Limbering-up Exercise

Sit on the floor with your legs spread wide apart. Without bending your knees, reach across your body with your left hand and touch the toes of your right foot. Then repeat the exercise, using the opposite hand and foot.

The Basic Side-Stretching Exercise

Stand straight with your feet about 8 or 10 inches (about 25 centimeters) apart. Place your left hand on your left hip, and bend your body sideways from the waist as far as it will go without strain. As you bend, arch your right arm over your head. Return to your original position and repeat the exercise, bending to the opposite side.

The Basic One-Arm Downward Stretch

Start from a standing position with your feet placed wide apart. Without bending your knees, reach down and touch your right foot with your left hand. Return to your original standing position. Then repeat the exercise, using the opposite hand and foot.

The Basic Balance Exercise

Stand straight with your feet together and your arms at your sides. Lean forward and raise one leg so that it is stretched straight out behind you. As you bend forward, extend your arms out to either side of your body. Hold this position for 10 seconds; then return to your original standing position. Repeat the exercise, raising your other leg.

The Basic One-Leg Stretch

Bend one knee deeply and extend the other leg straight out to your side. Using both hands (one on top of the other), push down gently on the upper thigh of the straightened leg. Then repeat the exercise, pressing on the opposite leg.

The Push-up Exercise

Begin by lying on your stomach with your arms bent, and your toes and knuckles resting on the floor. Raise your body off the floor by straightening your bent arms; then lower yourself back to your original position. (Keep your spine as straight as possible throughout the exercise.) This exercise should be done several times without stopping to rest.

The Basic Back Flexibility Exercise

Stand straight with your feet together and your hands on your hips. Keeping your knees straight, bend the top part of your body backward from the waist as far as you can without strain.

The Sit-up Exercise

Begin by lying flat on your back with your arms at your sides and your feet together. Raise the upper part of your body to a sitting position, and as you sit up, bring both arms forward and touch your toes. Return to your original position and repeat the exercise several times without stopping to rest.

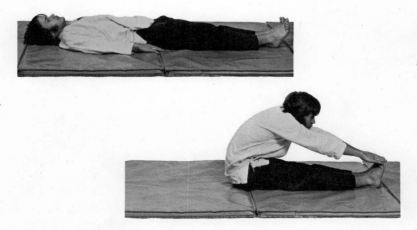

The Basic Flexibility Exercise

Stand in an upright, relaxed position, and slowly spread your legs as far apart as possible. At first, stretch your legs only as far as they will go without strain. If you do a little stretching each day, you will eventually be able to ease yourself all the way to the floor.

The Body Twisting Exercise

Stand with your legs apart and your knees slightly bent, and extend your arms straight out to either side. Twist your body at the waist as far to the left as you can. Then twist to the right.

The Muscle Tension Exercise

Stand straight with your feet wide apart, and place your right fist against the palm of your left hand. Push your fist against your palm with all your strength for a count of three; then relax. Repeat the exercise, pushing your left fist against your right palm.

The Front Bending Exercise

Stand straight with your legs placed slightly apart. Without bending your knees, reach down and touch the floor with the palms of your hands.

The Double Leg Raising Exercise

Lie on your back with your feet together and your hands folded under your head. Keeping both legs together, lift them slowly to a height of about two feet (60 centimeters) from the floor. Hold this position for 20 seconds. Next, lower your legs to a height of about three inches (7.5 centimeters) from the floor. Hold for 10 seconds. Then lower your legs slowly back to the floor.

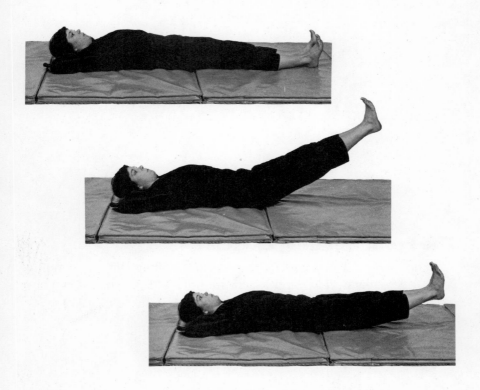

2.
STANCES FOR THROWING

Stances are special standing positions that are used in both judo matches and real self-defense situations. Some stances are defensive; they give your body stability and make it difficult for an opponent to off-balance or throw you. Other stances are offensive; they give your body flexibility and are used as starting positions for performing throws.

When you are learning the stances described in this chapter, you should practice them in front of a mirror. In this way, you can compare your body positions with those shown in the photographs. Each stance should be practiced until you can assume it almost automatically. When you have learned the individual stances, practice moving quickly from one stance to another. By shifting positions, you can take advantage of the special strengths of each particular stance.

The Basic Natural Stance

Face your opponent and stand erect with your feet placed 6 to 10 inches (about 25 centimeters) apart. Keep your shoulders relaxed, and let your arms rest comfortably at your sides. Your back should be straight, and your eyes should be focused directly on your opponent.

Basic

Right　　　　　　　　　　　　　　　　　　**Left**

The Right and Left Natural Stances

To assume a right natural stance, begin in the basic natural stance and simply place your right foot forward. For a left natural stance, place the left foot forward. When you are in either stance, the upper part of your body should face forward, and your weight should be evenly distributed between both legs.

NOTE: The natural stances are usually used as starting positions for performing throws. They are very comfortable, and you can maintain them for quite a long time without becoming tired. You can also shift easily to other body positions from these stances.

The Basic Self-Defense Stance

To assume the basic self-defense stance, stand straight and face your opponent. Place your legs almost two shoulder widths apart, with your knees bent and your weight evenly distributed between both legs. Your arms should be held in a comfortable position in front of your body.

Basic

Right   **Left**

The Right and Left Self-Defense Stances

Both of these stances begin from the basic self-defense stance. To assume a right self-defense stance, place your right foot ahead of your left. For a left self-defense stance, move the left foot forward. In both stances, your knees should remain deeply bent, and your body weight should be evenly distributed between both legs. The upper part of your body should face forward.

NOTE: The self-defense stances are solid and stable; therefore it is more difficult to move from these stances than it is to move from the natural stances. The self-defense positions should be used chiefly for defense against an opponent's attempt to off-balance or throw you.

MOVEMENT FROM THE THROWING STANCES

In addition to learning the stances, which help you to keep your balance when standing still, you must also learn how to maintain proper balance while moving. In order to stay balanced while moving, you must slide your feet as you step. If you slide, your body will be stable at all times, and it will be difficult for an opponent to throw you.

Generally, it is best to slide from one of the natural stances, because when you are in these stances, you are relaxed and can move more easily. This is important, because one of the keys to success in throwing is the ability to move quickly into a throw when an opportunity arises.

The Single-Foot Sliding Step

Learning Steps

1. Start in a basic natural stance.

2. Slide one foot forward, so that you end up in a right or left natural stance.

3. Be sure to keep your weight evenly distributed between both legs, so that your body is well balanced.

NOTE: To move backward, slide one foot to the rear instead of forward.

The Double-Foot Sliding Step

Learning Steps

1. Start in either a left or right natural stance, or in a left or right self-defense stance.

2. Slide your front foot forward. Then slide your back foot along behind, maintaining the original distance between your feet. Be sure to stay balanced as you move by keeping your weight evenly distributed between both legs.

NOTE: To move backward, slide your back foot to the rear, and follow with your front foot.

3.

FALLING TECHNIQUES

It is essential that students of the art of throwing learn how to fall properly when thrown by an opponent. Correct falling techniques have saved many people from being injured in a fight or a contest. In addition to preventing injury, knowledge of falling techniques also gives students a feeling of confidence, because they do not fear being thrown.

When you practice falling, you should always follow the safety rules listed below.

1. Always practice on a large, thick mat in order to protect yourself from injury. *Never* practice on a hard surface.

2. Always do the warm-up exercises before you begin falling, so that your body will be loose and flexible.

3. Do each fall slowly at first. This will give you a chance to develop good form. Do not speed up your movements until you have mastered the proper form.

The Side Fall

The side fall is the most commonly used falling technique in throwing. It is a very effective means of avoiding injury when you are thrown over an opponent's hip or shoulder. You can also use this fall when you are tripped, or when you are thrown by a leg sweep.

Learning Steps

1. Start in a squatting position, with one leg crossed just in front of the other.

2. Gradually slide your front leg forward. This sliding action should cause you to lose your balance and to fall on your side. As you fall, bring one arm up in the air.

3. Just before you hit the mat, beat the palm of your raised hand against the mat to break your fall.

NOTE: It is important that your body land properly, so that knees, ankles, and other sensitive spots are not injured. Make sure that after you land, your body is in the position illustrated in the last photo.

The Back Fall

This fall can be used when you are thrown or tripped so that you fall directly backward.

Learning Steps

1. Begin in a squatting position with your knees deeply bent. Extend your arms directly in front of your body, and tuck in your chin.

2. Spring up from the knees and allow your body to fall backward. As you fall, extend your arms out to either side of your body. (Your chin should remain securely tucked in so that your head does not hit the mat when you land.)

3. Just before your back hits the mat, break your fall by slapping your forearms against the mat about six inches (15 centimeters) from either side of your body.

NOTE: When you hit the mat, be sure that your body is in the position shown in the last photo. Your head should not touch the mat at any point during the fall.

The Front Fall

The front fall is useful when someone tackles you from behind. You can also use it any time that you slip and fall forward.

Learning Steps

1. Start in a kneeling position on the mat.

2. Rise up and let your body fall forward. Bring your arms up, with palms facing the mat.

3. When you fall, slap the mat with the palms of both hands to break your fall. Your stomach should not touch the mat at any point.

NOTE: It is very important that your hands and arms remain stationary after they slap the mat. They will support your body and will keep it from hitting the mat.

4.

THROWS FOR SPORT JUDO AND SELF-DEFENSE

This chapter describes a variety of throws that are generally accepted for use in sport judo. These throws are also effective techniques for practical self-defense. It is important to remember, however, that a judo contest can be very different from a real fight, and that you may have to adapt your use of each technique to your particular situation. In a judo contest, you know that your opponent will play by the rules and will "fight fair." In a real self-defense situation, however, your attacker most likely will not observe any rules at all. (For example, your opponent in a judo match will begin by facing you in a formal stance, whereas an attacker on the street may approach you from the back or side without warning.) Of course, you will need skill and adaptability to succeed in either a judo contest or a real fight. In a real fight, however, you must also be prepared to defend against opponents who use unexpected, and often unsportsmanlike, methods of fighting.

Whether you are using a throw for self-protection or sport judo, your chances of success will be greatest if you follow the four essential principles presented earlier in this book: get a firm grip on your opponent; make sure that your opponent's balance is broken before you attempt a throw; position your body properly before throwing; perform every step of the throw correctly and in one continuous motion.

In order to develop proper form, you should begin practicing alone, in front of a mirror. This way, you can compare your body positions and movements with those shown in the photographs. As you practice, try to imagine that you are throwing an actual opponent.

At some point, you will also need to practice with a partner. When you do so, it is very important that you keep in mind the following essential safety rules.

1. Always do all of the warm-up exercises before each practice session.

2. Always practice on a large, thick safety mat.

3. Do not practice throwing until you and your partner are sure that you both know how to fall properly.

4. Perform all throws as slowly and gently as possible when you are first learning.

5. Never try to "surprise" your partner—warn him or her before you attempt a throw.

OFF-BALANCING AN OPPONENT BEFORE THROWING

Before you try to throw an opponent in either a judo contest or a real fight, you must first break the opponent's balance. This will make your throw easier to perform, because an opponent who is off-balance will find it difficult to use his or her strength to stop you.

An aggressive opponent will often break his or her own balance simply by making the first move. For example, opponents who try to push you backward will usually off-balance themselves by putting their weight on the balls of their feet. They can easily be thrown forward, because their balance is already broken in that direction. Opponents who try to pull you forward usually off-balance themselves to the rear and can therefore be thrown backward quite easily.

There are situations, however, when an opponent is not off balance, even though he or she has made an aggressive move. In these situations, you must break the opponent's balance by pushing or pulling the person before attempting a throw. In the throws shown in this chapter, such off-balancing is usually done during the first two or three steps of the throwing technique.

When you are learning to off-balance an opponent, it is best to practice on a mat with a fellow student. During practice, try to keep the following helpful points in mind.

1. Always watch an opponent's stance carefully. You should attempt your throw at the exact moment when he or she is off balance.

2. Keep your body relaxed at all times, so that you can respond quickly when you see that an opponent is off balance.

3. Remember that an opponent is always easiest to throw in the direction in which he or she is moving.

4. If an opponent is not off balance, you can break the person's balance by directing his or her energy to your own advantage. If your opponent pushes, you should pull. If he or she pulls, then you should push.

The Two-Arm Shoulder Throw

This powerful throw is an effective technique for a short person to use against a tall opponent. This is because it is easy for a small person to perform one of the key steps of the throw—that of fitting one shoulder under the opponent's armpit.

Learning Steps

1. Face your opponent and step forward with your right foot, placing it directly in front of the opponent's right foot. Grip his or her right arm with your left hand. With your right hand, grasp the person's clothing at chest level.

2. Pivot on your right foot and step back with your left foot, so that your back is turned toward your opponent. As you pivot, maintain your grasp on his or her clothing. At the same time, pull the opponent's right arm up and forward, and fit your right arm under the person's armpit. Both of your knees should be deeply bent at this point.

3. To execute the throw, straighten your knees quickly, bend forward from the waist, and pull your opponent down onto the mat.

The One-Arm Shoulder Throw

This throw is a powerful defense against an opponent who moves forward to attack or throw you. Like the two-arm shoulder throw, it is an effective technique for a short person to use against a tall opponent.

Learning Steps

1. Begin in a basic natural stance, facing your opponent.

2. Place your right foot in front of the opponent's right foot. At the same time, grasp his or her right arm with your left hand.

3. Pivot on your right foot and step back with your left foot, so that your back is turned toward the opponent. (Both of your knees should be deeply bent when you reach this position.) As you pivot, pull the opponent's right arm forward and fit your right arm under his or her armpit. Grab the opponent's shoulder with your right hand. Now the opponent should be on your back, ready to be thrown.

4. To execute the throw, spring up from your bent-knee position, force your hips backward into the opponent's body, and pull the person forward over your shoulder.

The Basic Shoulder Whirl

This throw is a very good one to use if you want to catch an opponent off-guard.

Learning Steps

1. Start from a basic natural stance, facing your opponent, and grasp his or her inner right forearm with your left hand.

2. Pull down hard on the opponent's right arm to break his or her balance. As you pull, pivot on your left foot and let your right knee drop to the mat. (Your knee should rest between the opponent's feet.) With your right hand, reach between your opponent's legs and get a firm grip on the back of his or her right leg.

3. Continue to pull down on your opponent's right arm. As you pull, stand up with the person resting across your shoulders. (To avoid straining your back, use the strength of your leg muscles when performing this lift.)

4. To execute the throw, bend your body slightly to the left and drop your opponent onto the mat.

The Scooping Throw

This versatile throw can be used in many different situations. It is especially useful when an opponent has a strong hold on you.

Learning Steps

1. Begin in a basic natural stance, facing your opponent.

2. Pivot and swing your body around so that you are standing to the side of the opponent. Place your right foot behind the person's right foot, and your left foot to the outside of his or her left foot.

3. Bring your right arm across the front of the opponent's body and get a firm grip on the back of his or her right leg. At the same time, grab the person's left leg with your left arm.

4. To execute the throw, push your hips forward to off-balance the opponent, and lift his or her legs off the mat with your hands.

The Body-Drop Throw

This throw is a very effective response to an opponent who steps forward to attack or throw you.

Learning Steps

1. Begin in a right natural stance. Your left hand should grip your opponent's right arm, while your right hand grips the person's clothing at chest level.

2. When your opponent steps forward, pivot on your right foot and step back with your left foot, so that your back is turned toward the opponent. (Your left knee should be deeply bent.) As you turn, pull your opponent's right arm forward with your left hand, and pull up on his or her clothing with your right hand. These movements should off-balance the opponent in a forward direction.

3. Bend your right leg and place it across the front of your opponent's right leg. Your right foot should now be to the outside of the opponent's right foot, with toes pointing slightly inward.

4. To execute the throw, straighten out your right leg and pull down hard with your left hand, while you continue to push up with your right hand.

The Big Hip Throw

The big hip throw is one of the most basic throws in sport judo. It is most useful when an opponent is close to you and has a tight grip on your clothing. This throw may also be used when an opponent is trying to push you backward.

Learning Steps

1. Begin in a basic natural stance, and grasp your opponent's right arm with your left hand.

2. Place your right foot next to the inside of the opponent's right foot. At the same time, put your right arm around the opponent's waist.

3. Pivot on your right foot and step back with your left foot. The front of the opponent's body will now be resting against the back of your hip. At this point, your knees should be deeply bent and your toes pointed outward.

4. To execute the throw, spring up from your bent-knee position and pull the opponent forward over your hip.

The Rising Hip Throw

This throw is effective because it can be performed very rapidly, and can therefore be used to take an opponent by surprise.

Learning Steps

1. Begin in a basic natural stance, and grip your opponent's right arm with your left hand.

2. Step forward and place your right foot between your opponent's feet. As you do so, slip your right arm around the person's waist, and pull his or her right arm forward.

3. Pivot on your right foot and step back with your left foot. At the same time, pull the opponent's right arm across the front of your body. The opponent's body should now be resting tightly against your hip.

4. To execute the throw, twist your body slightly to the left and spring up on your toes as you pull the opponent over your hip.

The Lifting Hip Throw

This throw can be used in a variety of situations. It includes a lift-and-pull tactic that will effectively off-balance your opponent.

Learning Steps

1. Face your opponent and grip his or her right arm firmly with your left hand. With your right hand, grip the person's clothing at chest level and pull upward. Place your right foot in front of your opponent's right foot.

2. Pivot on your right foot and step back with your left foot, so that your back is turned toward the person. (At this point, both of your knees should be deeply bent.)

3. Continue to lift your opponent's clothing with your right hand while pulling his or her right arm forward. This lift-and-pull action should break the person's balance in a forward direction, so that his or her body is pulled up against your right hip.

Front view

4. To throw your opponent, straighten your bent knees and pull him or her over your hip.

The Hip Wheel Throw

This throw can be used for situations in which your opponent is off-balanced in a forward direction.

Learning Steps

1. Face your opponent and step forward with your right foot, so that it is directly in front of your opponent's right foot. At the same time, grasp his or her right arm with your left hand and pull it forward, alongside your upper body.

2. Now, pivot on your right foot and step back with your left foot. As you do so, hook your right arm around the back of the opponent's neck, and let the person's body rest against your hip. Make sure that both of your knees are deeply bent.

3. To execute the throw, straighten your knees and pull your opponent over your hip.

Front view

The Sweeping Hip Throw

This throw is an effective response to an opponent who steps forward to attack or throw you.

Learning Steps

1. Start in a right natural stance. When your opponent steps forward, grip his or her arm with your left hand. With your right hand, grasp the person's clothing at chest level.

2. Immediately pivot on your right foot and step back with your left foot. As you turn, pull the opponent's right arm forward with your left hand, and use your right hand to pull the opponent's body tight against your right hip.

3. Now, let most of your weight rest on your left leg for support, and stretch your right leg across the front of the opponent's right leg.

4. To throw your opponent, twist the upper half of your body to the left and sweep your right leg back forcefully. At the same time, pull the person's right arm to the left and downward across your body.

The Rear Lifting Throw

This is an excellent technique to use against an opponent who turns his or her back to you while attempting to throw you.

Learning Steps

1. When your opponent turns his or her back to you, bend your knees deeply, and quickly wrap your arms around the person's body.

2. To throw the opponent, straighten your knees and force your stomach up and forward into the opponent's body. (This will cause your upper body to snap backward.) At the same time, lift up and backward with your arms.

3. The combined action of snapping your upper body backward and lifting up with your arms should force the opponent to release his or her grip on you, and to fall backward to the mat.

The Outside Sweeping Leg Throw

This throw can be used any time that you are facing an aggressive opponent who is standing very close to you.

Learning Steps

1. Start in a basic natural stance, facing your opponent.

2. Step forward, placing your left foot near the outside of your opponent's right foot. At the same time, grab your opponent's right arm with your left hand and pull down, while pushing his or her body slightly backward with your other hand. These movements should break your opponent's balance to the rear.

3. Now, slip your right leg behind the opponent's right leg, so that the back of your leg is pressed tightly against the back of his or her leg.

4. To execute the throw, sweep your right leg behind you so that it takes the opponent's leg out from under him or her.

The Big Inside Sweeping Leg Throw

This is a very powerful technique to use when an opponent is standing close to you with feet placed wide apart.

Learning Steps

1. Begin by facing your opponent. Then grasp both of your opponent's arms and push backward in order to break his or her balance to the rear.

2. Twist your right hip forward and place your right leg between the opponent's legs, so that your foot rests behind his or her left foot.

3. To execute the throw, continue pushing the opponent backward. Then sweep the person's left leg out from under him or her with the back of your right leg.

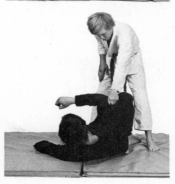

The Outside Heel Sweep

This throw is very effective for situations in which your opponent steps forward with the right foot to attempt a throw.

Learning Steps

1. Start from a basic natural stance, with your left hand gripping your opponent's right arm, and your right hand grasping his or her clothing at chest level.

2. When your opponent steps forward with his or her right foot, step around to the person's right side with your left foot.*

3. To break your opponent's balance to the rear, pull the person's right arm downward and toward his or her body while you push the person backward with your right hand.

4. At the same time, bend your left leg and place the sole of your foot against the back of the opponent's right heel. To complete the throw, sweep the opponent's foot forward so that he or she falls to the mat.

*NOTE: It is important that you act at the exact moment when your opponent is shifting weight to his or her right foot.

The Inside Sweeping Heel Throw

You can use this technique to throw an aggressive opponent who steps forward with the right foot to attack or throw you.

Learning Steps

1. Start from a right natural stance, with your left hand gripping the opponent's right elbow and your right hand grasping his or her clothing at chest level.

2. When the opponent steps forward with his or her right foot, step back with your left foot and turn so that you are standing with your right side toward the person. Place the sole of your right foot against the back of the opponent's right heel.

3. To throw the opponent, pull his or her right arm downward, and push back on the person's chest. At the same time, sweep the opponent's heel toward your left, so that he or she falls backward onto the mat.

The Basic Foot Sweep

This is an excellent technique for catching an opponent off-guard. It is most often used to counterattack a person who steps forward in an attempt to throw you.

Learning Steps

1. Begin in a basic self-defense stance, facing your opponent.

2. When the opponent steps forward, grip both of his or her arms and place the sole of your left foot against the outside of the person's right heel.*

3. To execute the throw, pull down hard on the opponent's arms and sweep the person's right foot toward your right, so that he or she falls to the mat.

*NOTE: To do this throw correctly, you must act at the exact moment when your opponent shifts his or her weight by stepping forward.

The Outside Whirl Throw

This technique is very effective against an opponent who tries to resist a forward throw by leaning backward.

Learning Steps

1. Start in a right natural stance, with your left hand gripping the opponent's right elbow and your right hand grasping the person's clothing at chest level.

2. Pull your opponent toward you, as though you are attempting a forward throw. When the person leans backward to resist, step forward with your left foot, placing it to the outside of his or her right foot. Stretch your right leg across the back of the opponent's legs.

3. To throw the opponent backward, pull down with your left hand and push back with your right hand. At the same time, sweep the person's legs upward with your right leg.

Front view

The Falling Circle Throw

This is a good technique to use against a large, aggressive opponent who tries to push you backward.

Learning Steps

1. Start in a natural stance, with your hands tightly gripping your opponent's clothing at chest level.

2. Give your opponent a hard push, maintaining your grip on the clothing. When he or she responds by pushing you backward, quickly stretch your left foot forward and place it between the person's legs.

3. Bend your left knee and drop on your back to the mat. As you drop, bring your right foot up and place it against the opponent's lower stomach. At the same time, pull down hard with both hands.

4. To throw your opponent, straighten your right leg and continue to pull down with your arms until the person is thrown over your head and onto the mat.

5.
THROWS FOR SELF-DEFENSE

All of the throws presented in the preceding chapter are suitable for both sport judo and self-defense. There are many other throwing techniques, however, that are not an official part of sport judo. Although these techniques are not permitted in a judo contest, they are excellent methods of practical self-defense. The throws in this chapter are effective responses to punching or grabbing attacks made by a real-life aggressor. Each throw is designed to counter a particular kind of attack, and each throw is combined with practical blocking and escaping techniques. If you practice each technique thoroughly, you will be able to respond quickly and efficiently in many self-defense situations. (To practice these techniques safely with a partner, follow the safety rules suggested in Chapter 4 of this book.)

The Lifting Leg Throw

This throw can be used when an attacker comes up behind you and grabs you around the waist.

Learning Steps

1. When someone grabs you around the waist, immediately assume the basic self-defense stance and bend slightly forward.

2. Next, beat hard on the backs of the attacker's hands with your knuckles to loosen the person's grip.

3. When the attacker's grip loosens, quickly bend down, reach between your legs, and grab the person's ankle.

4. Pull the ankle up forcefully, so that the attacker falls backward onto the ground.

The Rear Leg Sweep

This throw is most often used to counterattack an aggressor who throws a punch at you.

Learning Steps

1. Begin in a right natural stance, facing your attacker.

2. When the attacker throws a right-hand punch, quickly raise your right arm to meet his or her punching arm. Block the intended punch with the outside edge of your forearm.

3. Immediately after you have blocked the punch, grab the aggressor's right arm with your right hand. At the same time, shift your body weight to your right foot and bend your left arm so that the elbow points toward the aggressor.

4. To throw the attacker, snap your left arm out straight so that it strikes his or her chest. At the same time, sweep the person's right leg forward with your left leg.

The Side Kick Throw

The side kick throw can be used to counterattack a forceful punching attack to the head.

Learning Steps

1. Begin in a basic natural stance, facing your attacker.

2. When the aggressor throws a right-hand punch at you, dodge it by stepping quickly to the side with your left foot and bending your body to the left. At the same time, grasp the attacker's punching arm with your right hand.

3. Next, bend your right leg and kick the back of the aggressor's right knee with the sole of your foot, so that his or her leg is swept forward. At the same time, pull down hard on the aggressor's punching arm with your right hand. If these movements are done correctly, the person should fall backward onto the ground.

The Lifting Leg Trip

This technique is useful when an aggressor is close to you and tries to grab you.

Learning Steps

1. If an aggressor puts his or her hands on your shoulders, bend forward and grab the back of the person's right leg with your left hand.

2. As you lift the aggressor's leg off the ground, step between the person's legs with your right foot, and place your right leg behind his or her left leg. The back of your right leg should now be pressed tightly against the back of the aggressor's left leg.

3. To execute the throw, push the aggressor backward with your right hand while you continue to lift his or her right leg off the ground. At the same time, kick the aggressor's left leg out from under him or her with your right leg.

The Double Leg Throw

This throw can be used any time that an aggressor is facing you and tries to grab you.

Learning Steps

1. Begin in a basic natural stance. When your attacker reaches forward to grasp your shoulders, bend down quickly, step forward with your right foot, and butt the person's stomach with your head.

2. At the same time, grasp the aggressor's legs behind the knees, and pull up and forward. The aggressor will then fall backward to the ground.

SAFETY RULES

When you practice throwing techniques with a partner, you must always be sure to take proper safety precautions. Remember that a practice session is not a competitive situation, but a time when you and your partner can work together to improve your skills. If you follow the safety rules listed below, you will reduce the likelihood of injury, and your practice sessions will be both safe and effective.

1. Always practice falls and throws on a large, thick safety mat.

2. Limber up before each practice session by doing the complete sequence of warm-up exercises.

3. Perform all falls and throws as slowly and carefully as possible when you are first learning.

4. Do not practice throwing until you and your partner are sure that you both know how to fall properly.

5. Never try to "surprise" your partner—warn him or her before you attempt a throw.

INDEX

ABOUT THE AUTHOR

Fred Neff has been a student of the Asian fighting arts for most of his life. He started his training at the age of eight and eventually specialized in karate. Today Mr. Neff holds the rank of fifth degree black belt in that fighting art. In addition to karate, he is also proficient in judo and jujitsu. For many years, Mr. Neff has used his knowledge of the Asian fighting arts to educate others. He has taught karate at the University of Minnesota, the University of Wisconsin, and Hamline University and Inver Hills College in St. Paul, Minnesota. He has also organized and supervised self-defense classes in public schools, private schools, and in city recreation departments. Included in his teaching program have been classes for law enforcement officers.

Fred Neff graduated with high distinction from the University of Minnesota College of Education in 1970. In 1976, he received his J.D. degree from William Mitchell College of Law in St. Paul, Minnesota. Mr. Neff is now a practicing attorney in Minneapolis, Minnesota.